MASS
DESIGN

CONTENTS

KOERT VAN MENSVOORT
PP. 51–63

KOEN VERMEIR
PP. 65–110

FLORIAN SCHNEIDER
PP. 31–50

CHAT
PP. 5–30

FREEK LOMME **KOERT VAN MENSVOORT** **FLORIAN SCHNEIDER** **VAN ABBEMUSEUM (AUDITORIUM)**

CHAT

Hallo Koert!
           hallo Freek
prima!
Design Mass
Challenging the technocratic state of design.
Will start soon!
Take a seat!
           hi
           hello world
Hi other world!
Koert: shall we start: please stop talking!
pay attention please!
KOERT!
Is this our digital community?
o.k.: welcome everyone!
           hello!
welcome to TAKE ON ME (TAKE ME ON)
Let me give you a brief introduction, before we go to Florian Schneieder and Koert van Mensvoort

FL　　　　　KVM　　　　FS　　　　　VAM

Design Mass is a project by Onomatopee, hosted here in the museum
technocratic system of the neo-liberal design industry offer after the crisis and how can they bring this forth?
The technological deterministic prophesy of design is challenged. What could the technocratic system of the neo-liberal design industry offer after the crisis and how can they bring this forth?
Our welfare state implements humanist norms and values through a direct connection of the new, labour and salary. This system fulfilled itself within the commodity. Our shared religion remains neoliberal, based on the consumption of identity.
We often indulge ourselves into these promises, promising ourselves a better future (beyond the credit crisis).
The current western consumption culture is in decay. The commodity-culture became obsolete, cannot cultivate anymore: cannot gain sales, cannot pay off its production. The resulting physical domain of produced commodities grows on and on like a cancer. Even though in decay, this highly technocratic system remains to put forth new products with new promises. An ongoing outcome of technical progress enables the ongoing production of new products 'unlike ever experienced before'. An ongoing outcome of technical progress still lures us by means

of marketing. Most of all, the religious sphere of the commodity became an obsolete fraud, since it cannot not sell its religious promise of humanistic fulfilment anymore. Globalism, the final free-market, only showcased the decadence of the western world: we're not needed! The western neo-liberal system needs to reposition their production and promises.

Big design events, like the Dutch Design Week, flourish as never before. These events celebrate an enlightened promise of progress while western progress might not be able to cope with the material progress that dominated since the start of the industrial revolution. How does our culture, how do you and me relate to this event? How can we comprehend and cope with it; what does it offer and what could it release? How does this technocratic state relate to the flexibility of our culture?

Onomatopee challenges the parameters of our (visual) culture. For the Dutch Design Week 2009, their gallery space will be overturned into a space of contemplation and reflection. Onomatopee invites theoreticians/writers known with the field of technological culture and design, to contemplate within the celebration, to reflect on its parameters and target groups from the perspective of the targeted themselves. Operating from within the event itself, located in a public accessible

FL KVM FS VAM

office at Onomatopee's gallery space, they will be directly in contact with the targeted and the events technocratic body: its creators and mediators.
so: we're situated here, in this digital sphere, niceley together, to think further and think beyond the frame of current design... maybe...
Florian: when you were confronted with our question, how was your first response and what did you came up with so far?

> first of all i want to thank you for the invitation!
> i am really happy to be here

you're welcome!

> for a few very particular reasons
> very often when i get invited to give a talk in a similar situation
> i find my self confronted with a paradox
> i am trying to prepare, write a peper etc.
> but only after the talk itself, i feel like i finally know what i should have been talking about
> so i am really very glad to be part of

FL   **KVM**   **FS**   **VAM**

> an experiment that
> turns this separation
> between the actual
> production of a text
> and its presentation
> upside down
> and i am looking fwd
> very much
> the questions you have
> been raising are truly
> very important ones

{I recognize that Florian, I have that too}

Florian: when we first spoke you mailed me some ideas, i quote:'the significance of the separation between manual labor and intellectual labor in digital environments like contemporary design.'
sorry: clicked enter to fast...

> after i received the
> invitation to take part
> in this project i have
> been quite intrigued
> by the question of
> determinism. but i
> would like to try to mis-
> understand it slightly
> yes

but: did that still interest you?

> absolutely
> i would come up with
> the following proposal:

FL   **KVM**   **FS**   **VAM**

FS: its not the technological development that is determinig how we work and live but precisely our very understanding of it that determines it.

KVM: is it a mind set?

FS: for instance our understanding how to deal with so-called manual and so-called intellectual labor seems to me not just a determining but a rather constitutive element.
so what i thought i would like to work on (and this is just a beginning of a maybe much larger project) is the question: how does that separation between manual and intellectual labor appear in times of post-industrial capitalism
which is usually considered as an immaterial economy,

FL   **KVM**   **FS**   **VAM**

knowledge economy, creative industries etc. as if there were no manual labor anymore, and everything were intellectual, creative, imaginary etc.

i have the suspicion that instead we are confronted with a total reorganization of the very same idea of separating so-called brainwork from work with our hands

in my research i came across a very interesting figure

a german philosopher, who never really published a book until the very end of his life

he was a good friend of adorno, part of the early frankfurt school, but then had to emigrate to britain where he spent his live as a german teacher in birmingham

at the funeral of adorno he came back

FL   **KVM**   **FS**   **VAM**

>to germany and met siegfried unseld, the famopus publisher who asked him what happened to his plans to write a book that re-reads marx with kant (as opposed to hegel) in the few years before his death alfred sohn-rether then wrote this book and it got pubslihed in the early 70s under the title: <u>manual and intellectual labor</u>
>my project would be, to-re-read this book, which cerrtainly deals with the separating between manual and intellectual labor in the age of industrial capitalism and then figure out what has actually changed

Can you share a speculation on what you think has changed Florian?

>what are the main characteristics of a cognitive capitalism

> as it is presented to us today, as opposed to fordist, industrial production.
> with pleasure ;)

But didn't this book play indeed in a different era? I'm just thinking out silently: is the labor our material order, or might it not be well-being?

> yes, that is for example what michael hardt (and toni negri) suggested in empire: the production is no longer about tangible material products, but rather about well-being... i see their point, i agree with them, but i have increasing doubts whether this captures the crucial point...
> now that we have experienced lets say 10–15 years of digital production
> let me briefly come back to sohn-rethel and his (truly outdated) analysis.

(y)

FL   KVM   FS   VAM

he identifies the process of 'real abstraction' that characerizes the commodity form and the exchange as the crucial point, since it corresponds also with the epistemoligical implications of a philosophical tradition that understands thinking as a product of thinking and ultimately seperates between theory and practice.
accortding to S-R the abstraction of exchange in industrial capitalism is characterized by 4 aspects
1. practical solipsism of the exchangers: those who excchange meet as loners, the act of exchange modifies ownership but not the domain of property itself
2. the act of exchange postulates the absolute material constancy of the commodity

FL   KVM   FS   VAM

3. a-syncronicity of exchange and use
4. abstract singularity of the commodity which consitutes its form of exchangeability
if we take these four points and critical discuss how the situation is today we will probably realize that the exact opposite comes true
nevertheless capitalism is still there, we are living in a commidity-based economy and the commidity form is fetishized to an extent that is almost not recognizable anymore
the results are the same but the preconditions seems to change dramatically
1. there is absolutely no loniliness in times of social networking and community based production

FL　　　　KVM　　　　FS　　　　VAM

> 2. in the digital realm there is a prevalent material inconsistency and impermanence of the objects to be exchanged
> 3. exchange and use happen at least near on real time: the temporal implosion of use and exchange
> 4. the multiplicity of the commodity constitutes its exchangeability
> so, against this backdrop i am wondering how that may affect the separation of manual and intellectual labor for example in digital graphic design, in contemporary image production as such

there's no such thing as Danto's last artist being a phlosopher? back to the material? can concepts be applied at all? especially in regard of the crisis? Can we only escape in weird commnities like the one we're in now?

> i just read a very interesting piece by bruno

14:34:54　　　　CHAT – 16

FL   **KVM**   **FS**   **VAM**

latour last night
he writes about a
constant de- and
re-materialization
that characterizes for
instance scrientific
research/scientific
or more concretely: is
the programmer who
is writing the code
for an application
considered a manual
laborer?
what about the cleaners who are cleaning
the office space
(and truly produce
well-being rather
than a clean space)

I think the border between manual and intellectual labor isn't
the important thing to consider.

security guards, software developers etc.
@koert: why do you
think?

Intellectual labor used to be associated with more freedom and
room for creativity, but it is the
question if this is till the case.
We were looking at the film Objectified
yesterday; Gary Huswith's new film on

14:38:27   CHAT – 17

FL   **KVM**   **FS**   **VAM**

designing. Designing seemed to become the new policy; operating through minimalist aesthetics and dito/effective useability. The promise brought about seemed to entail technological prgress: human progress the new organic outcome...

> Many of the intellectual workers, knowledge workers today are also just workin within the parameters given to them...

their labor, the designers labor, was becoming more and more speculative... while the execution of the work was plain work...

> @Freek... havent seen that movie.
>> so that could mean that the original separation between manual and intellectual labor that once had divided classes today is transformed into an individual schizophrenia each of us has to deal with...

well: the movie is kind of dull, but says a lot about the regular 'top-class' designsphere

> Perhaps this relates to the difference between 'ontwerpers' and 'vormgevers' we have in the Netherlands... (designers vs form-tweekers')

A digital alienation?

FL	KVM	FS	VAM

          i am afraid it goes way beyond alienation...

do-ers and thinkers extending their bodies with electrones hovering through the air?

          Freek, I don't get exactly what you mean by alienation... It is such a general word.

it was a stupid sentence indeed: realized that to late...

                    @koert: is this separation between 'developers' and 'executers' still valid today?

          @Florian: I sense we are ariving at a conclusiong that the separation between 'developers' and 'executers' is perhaps still valid, however it is no longer related to whether you are working 'in material' or 'in an office'.

                    sure!
                    but the strange thing is that those who wrote the code of photoshop are formatting to a large extent what those who are supposed to 'develop' are actually able to design...
                    same for so-called web-design. i am

FL   **KVM**   **FS**   **VAM**

            very interested in the concrete relationships between designers and coders, for example

Agreed... again, here we see a seperation between 'designers' and 'form-tweekers'
Where programmers certainly can be 'designers' in this case.

            yes, but this separation which kind of echoes the ancient separation between manual and intellectual labor (labor that commands and labor that obeys) is getting more and more twisted

mediated?

            @Florian, you say it twisted, but isn't it merely a simple rotation? And I'd say a good one too!

            to be honest, i do not see a lot of mediation, rather despotic modes of command and control, at leats in commercial and corporate environments. at the same time it is very interesting to analyze larger

FL **KVM** **FS** **VAM**

> groups of open source developers how they deal with that problem...
> i would say its twisted since the relationship becomes more and more complicated

This relates to what I've been studing this week.
Which is the development of Gillette Razors over time. :)

> great!

please elaborate!

> I've looked at all the razors I have bought since my first shave (when I was fifteen)
> My first razor consisted of two blades on a simple metal stick and I remember it gave me a really close and comfortable shave.
> This morning I shaved myself with the "Gillette Fusion Power Phantom", a rather heavy, yet ergonomically designed battery-powered razor that looks like a bit like vacuum cleaner and has six vibrating knifes with an aloe strip for moisture.
> No thats progress folks?!
> Throughout my life I've bought over 12 different razors (I admit,

FL   KVM   FS   VAM

I am keen on new things: a sucker for innovation)

> yes, i can confirm. and i think it really got much better over time

Well, yes... it got better, although it also got kind of excessive don't you think?

totally excessive!

Actually already in 1975, shortly after the Gillette Trac II razor—the first two-bladed men's razor, known as Contour in many parts of the world—was advertized, the excessive design of these razors was parodied on the US Television show Saturday Night Live. The creators of the satirical TV program played on the idea of a two bladed razor as a sign of the emerging consumption culture and made a fake commercial parody for a fictitious razor with the ridiculous amount of three (!) blades.

> so how does this related to a manual shave in a barber shop made by a professional barber with a long knife?

Good question... perhaps that is

FL   **KVM**   **FS**   **VAM**

> a retro-movement that is being made now (if we are ready for it). Although first let me elaborate a bit on the development of razors in my lifetime.
> If you look at the development of the razors you can lean a lot about design, technology, market and perhaps even evolution.
> Especially in the last decade you see a shift from functional technologies, like the pivoting head on the razor, to functionless aesthetics of the newer models, that sometimes only change in color, which remind of the exuberant tail of a male peacock
> Utterly useless, but it works fine as a survival strategy.

survival in/for?

> Well, what can I say... I bought all these razors...

I bought an electronic razer a few weeks ago since i wanted to shave in the morning while taking a shower: the divice is shitty, doesn't work so again i shave to less but with simple wet mechanics...

so, from the perspective of the user/consumer/hir/hers responsability: is the techological promise in the eye of te beholder, or is it really a fundamental thing?

> @Freek: I think: both.

FL   **KVM**   **FS**   **VAM**

> me too
> I already gave the example of the tail of a peacock. That is a useless, but also beautiful thing, I appreciate that (after all, I bought all these useless razors).

Well: we can debate personal taste, but how about our nature/our being: when we speak about our nature, to what extend is it natural?

> @Freek: First we have to look at the 'designers' and 'engineers' who are creating these new razors every year (and this relates to the beginning of our discussion). What more are these people than little cogs in the perpetuating Gillette corporation? Calling them engineers and designers is actually too much credit for the work they do, as they are no more than technicians and form tweekers instructed by the marketing department.
> Like bees in a beehive their work is determined by the logic of the larger structure. The Gillette designers—as we will call them—have not much room for truly created design to study the meaning and the origins of shaving.
>> natural would be not to shave at all, since

FL	KVM	FS	VAM

> **FS:** it is a useless thing as such. so it becomes a classical example of when the goal of production is well-being rather than something substantial... here, when the use value seems to be almost neglectable designers and developers are facing different kind of challenges that are extremely interesting imho

> **VAM:** Interesting point of view, Freek. And we did not even talk about environmental sustainability...

> **FS:** Yes, so now you know why the Taliban have beards.

> **FS:** @Koert: is the producer the creator of our world?

> **VAM:** No, that I would be way to much credit. Rather as I see it, things co-evolve.

FL	KVM	FS	VAM

    I think the metaphor of the bees and there beehive can be helpful here.

But that might relate to the type of abstraction Florian brought about... when he spoke of the post-industrial?

    Looking at that from the metaphor of the bees and their beehive, that would mean something like the life of bees, after their beehive has crashed?
    Of course, there is a difference between people and bees. As bees can be lured into almost anything, whereas people...

o.k... i'm getting diffused now, yet inspired: maybe some last words? (i'd maybe like to include this weird talk into the booklet we'll be publishing...)

Don't know if our audience has any questions: there's a laptop vacant besides the entrance!

If we dont distinguish between manual and intellectual labour anymore, what do we distinguish then? I didnt get it.

    Ok... some last words. I think people are different than bees, we should be able to reflect on the direction we are going as a society.
        i can only agree and i see the alleged uselessness of razor

FL   **KVM**   **FS**   **VAM**

> design paradigmatic for major parts of these so-called creative industries whose purpose seems to be to be as harmless as possible in order to proliferate as much as possible.

I think you have 'gillette designers', who are merely operating within the existing beehive and do their job. Fine. But their is also still room and need for creative people who question the parameters of the system they are in and start working from that.

> Using a chat-text. I notice two consequences: 1. Development of multiple threads (increased complexity) 2. slower pace of discussion. What are

FL	KVM	FS	VAM

                                    the benefits? Why has this format been chosen?

                        but i would like to add that i am interested in something that matters and has the capacity to possibly change a given situation...

                                      I guess for people like me... I can read it and understand it better... some things take some time to sink in.

i thought the format might be wortwhile, since it offert room to reflect before you type. As well, this type of incrouwd communication might illustrate how we produce/live...
that was in response to VAMAUDITORIUM
maybe i can get this printed in a sec:
for al of you

                              @freek: i guess that is very true and i have

FL   **KVM**   **FS**   **VAM**

to confess that besides using gilettes fusion power every second morning i spend two thirds of my working day in chat interfaces.

I think we can regard this chat as an experiment as well: can we really cumulativeley build knowlegde in direct exchange: face to face we might find more pschycollogical affirmation...
good to gain friction, to know that you've said a lot, that Koert brought forth all these topics: appreciate that very much!
so: to end up the conversation
if you'd like to receive a handout of this chat say YES now!

What I like about this form is that it is so quiet and yet so full of ideas and opinions. As if we all are in one big virtual brain...

i like that to: could go on for ages!

FL   **KVM**   **FS**   **VAM**

Fascinating, yet also a bit daunting...
Ok thanks everyone...
thank you
                thank you!
as well: you can visit the DESIGN MASS at Onomatopee: we've created a study over there, where texts can be checked up.
With texts by: Koert, the man on my right side, Florian, on my left side and Koen vermeir, currently in Zurich!
thanks to Remco for the exhibition design over there!
tomorrow, Objectified will be screened and discussed in this space, at 14:00
thank you!

FLORIAN SCHNEIDER

NOTES ON THE DIVISION OF LABOR

DISCLAIMER

The following is neither a fully comprehensive analysis nor a finally thought-through elaboration of the topic of the division of labor.

It should rather be understood as a survey offering a platform for further research, discussion and development. It reflects the results of a series of explorations into a topic that is extensive and might turn out as being of considerable relevance.

...

In 1931, the Philips corporation from Eindhoven commissioned the first Dutch sound movie. <u>Philips Radio</u> or <u>Industrial Symphony</u> is a documentary by Joris Ivens produced at the peak of the economic depression and at the advent of the breakthrough of radio technology for a mass market.

The 36' movie was supposed to show the modern production process of radios in the factories and offices of Philips in Eindhoven. What we see is a celebration of images, that aims to recompose the industrial division of labor as an artwork.

The fascination by the abstract beauty of the mechanic processes on one hand, and the concrete portrayal of the hard work that is carried out by the workers on the other, constitute a cinematic piece whose ambiguity was irritating for both its client and the majority of critics.

The corporation reportedly refused to show the movie in its original version, while the Christian newspaper <u>Het Volk</u> considered it to be a "document of inhumanity". According to the critics, Ivens did not expose the assembly line as a subjugation of the worker to the rule of the machine in the same way as Chaplin did in the famous opening sequence of <u>Modern Times</u> or René Clair in a strikingly similar scene of his <u>À nous la liberté!</u>

Rather than a caricature, Ivens intended to depict the "cinematic expression of a, rather <u>the</u> twentieth century production line manufacturer." The movie's non-complicity, its avoidance of the cliches of both advertising the success of the company and mere anti-technological propaganda, may constitute its rather unexpected contemporary value.

Eyal Sivan, who selected the movie in 2009 for the documentary film festival in Amsterdam as part of several screenings of his favorite documentary movies, writes:

> "Instead of a valiant movie parade through all the departments, he reveals the working conditions in a modern mechanized factory and captures the step-by-step development of radio parts along the way."

What is at stake is the precise depiction of a division of labor: the specialization of labor that is necessary in order to sell a product — by the time when the movie was made already more than 100 millions of vacuum tubes.

Ivens shows the entire chain from advanced glassblowing techniques to the assembly of complete radios, from the research laboratories to the typing rooms with hundreds of secretaries and the packaging of the radio set.

...

"Division of labor" is a concept that has been first systematically explored by William Petty, whom Karl Marx considered to be "the founding father of political economy". Petty observed enthusiastically how in the course of the 18th century, the specialization in the manufacturing of cloth and watches and shipping was supposed to increase overall productivity by its cheapening effects:

> "Cloth must be cheaper made, when one Cards, another Spins, another Weaves, another Draws, another Dresses, another Presses and Packs; then when all the operations above mentioned were clumsily performed by the same hand."

> "In the making of a Watch, If one Man should make the Wheels, another the

Spring, another shall Engrave the Dial-Plate, and another shall make the Cases, then the Watch will be better and cheaper than if the whole Work be put upon any one Man."

Petty tried to explain the material basis of the contrast between Dutch economical success and poverty in Ireland. In fact, he applied the principle of the division of labor which he experienced in shipyards in the Netherlands to his survey of Ireland by putting into practice the very notion of a division of scientific labor. He split up the statistical tasks into what could be easily done by unskilled soldiers and what would need professional attention.

...

On the 13 March 2007 the Bank of England issued a new style 20 Pound note as a replacement for the old one with portrait of Sir Edward Elgar on the back. Along with a different "look" of the note, the main change was the inclusion of a portrait of Adam Smith on the back of the note, along with the image of a pin-producing factory and a summary of Smith's observations on the benefits of the division of labor, drawn from his major work, <u>An Inquiry into the Nature and Causes of the Wealth of Nations</u>, commonly referred to as <u>The Wealth of Nations.</u>

In the famous example of a pin factory, Smith explained how cooperation between workers in the factory, dividing the tasks among each other, raised their combined output. He continued to explain how, by trading with others, both at home and abroad, we could specialize our own production, and how society as a whole would benefit from higher incomes and standards of living. The banknote depicts the division of labour in the pin factory, and features a caption borrowed from <u>The Wealth of Nations</u>: "and the great increase in the quantity of work that results".

"To take an example, therefore, from a very trifling manufacture; but one in which the division of labour has been very often taken notice of, the trade of the pin-maker; a workman not educated to this business (which the division of labour has rendered a distinct trade), nor acquainted with the use of the machinery employed in it (to the invention of which the same division of labour has probably given occasion), could scarce, perhaps, with his utmost industry, make one pin in a day, and certainly could not make twenty. But in the way in which this business is now carried on, not only the whole work is a peculiar trade, but it is divided into a number of branches, of which the greater part are likewise peculiar trades. One man draws out the wire, another straights it, a third cuts it, a fourth points it, a fifth grinds it at the top for receiving, the head; to make the head requires two or three distinct operations; to put it on is a peculiar business, to whiten the pins is another; it is even a trade by itself to put them into the paper; and the important business of making a pin is, in this manner, divided into about eighteen distinct operations, which, in some manufactories, are all performed by distinct hands, though in others the same man will sometimes perform two or three of them."

...

"The average man in a communist society would be able to go fishing in the morning, work in a factory in the afternoon and read Plato in the evening." According to best-selling author Alain de Botton, Karl Marx must have imagined communist utopia as an "implausibly high-minded combination of activities".

Within one single working day one would enjoy unhurried peasant lifestyle, benefit from the efficiency of industrial production and then turn to the blessings of brainwork. In such an idyllic scenario communism would be anything but boring.

As a celebration of the whole variety of human capacities, communism would mark the unification of body and mind in an integral approach. And isn't it precisely the case that what 19th century Marx is supposed to describe as a utopia, has today become reality for a growing number of highly skilled workers, namely those working in the "creative industries"?

There is just one little problem. The quote which the author, who is most recently responsible for projects with titles like like <u>The School of Life</u>, assigned to what he calls the "concluding volume" of <u>Capital</u> is an invention of Botton himself.

Unfortunately, Marx has not made any remark like the above in any of the volumes of <u>Capital</u>. Instead, there are remarkably different lines in "The German Ideology", a book he wrote thirty years earlier:

> "In communist society, where nobody has one exclusive sphere of activity but each can become accomplished in any branch he wishes, society regulates the general production and thus makes it possible for me to do one thing today and another tomorrow, to hunt in the morning, fish in the afternoon, rear cattle in the evening, criticise after dinner, just as I have a mind, without ever becoming hunter, fisherman, herdsman or critic."

Marx never dared to give any further hint about how one should imagine communism, even though he became permanently pressured by the growing proletarian movement to reveal his vision of a communist utopia. Marx refused a religious, utopian notion of communism and insisted instead on the "scientific" character of his research.

Indeed, much more interesting than the distribution of concrete practices between hunting, fishing and herding plus some criticism after work is the rather abstract thought that comes after that:

"This fixation of social activity, this consolidation of what we ourselves produce into an objective power above us, growing out of our control, thwarting our expectations, bringing to naught our calculations, is one of the chief factors in historical development up till now."

...

In the first volume of "Das Kapital" Karl Marx has introduced a sharp distiction between a division of labor that is a technical or economic division of labor and that is supposed to increase efficiency in the process of co-operation.

But then he also identified a social division of labor that is socially constructed. The result is a double division of labor:
- the technical division of labor in the enterprise and in a particular industry that broke down the production process into a sequence of tasks and
- the social division of labor among enterprises, industries, and social classes that was mediated through commodity exchange in market relations.

Division of labor appears as a double relation along two axes or "connections" whose specific combination constitutes the historical uniqueness of a mode of production (Althusser and Balibar in "Reading Capital"):
1 A relation of real appropriation designates the structure of the labor process, that is, the relation of the laborer to the means of production by which the transformation of

nature is undertaken. This relation constitutes the "technical division of labor" or the forces of production.
2 A property relation designates the mode of appropriation of the social product. This relation, the "social division of labor" or relations of production, implies the intervention of an individual or a collectivity, who, by the exercise of economic ownership, controls access to the means of production and the reproduction of the productive forces.

...

The success of Ford's model T ("a motor car for the great multitude") was made possible by the introduction of a new factory system that characterizes first of all a new technical division of labor.

It was based on an enormous increases of
- precision: only interchangeable parts were used in manufacturing
- specialisation: breaking up the assembly of a car into 84 distinct steps
- synchronization: A minimum time spent in set-up between these steps. motion studies by Frederick Taylor had to determine the exact speed at which the work should proceed and the exact motions workers should use to accomplish their tasks.

The Model T was the first automobile mass produced on assembly lines with completely interchangeable parts. Machines were used to reduce complexity of the production process in 84 areas in order to streamline the assembly process of a car from 12.5 hours to 93 minutes. Instead of skilled craftsmen, low-skilled or untrained workers were hired who needed skills and knowledge in only one of the 84 areas.

At the same time Fordism has triggered a dramatic expansion a new social division of labor from what was by then called productive to reproductive work: Workers are not only supposed to produce products at a much greater efficiency, but due to relative high wages, they were at the same time targeted as consumers. The intensification and differentiation of the production process is partly compensated by increasing amounts of free time and higher wages that in the return had to be spent for the consumption of the same products.

The intensification of the labor process was accompagnied by the moral regulation of the private lives of workers. Work and non-work life became increasingly linked up. In his famous text on "Americanism and Fordism" Gramsci argues that the new methods of work are inseparable from a specific mode of living and of thinking and feeling life.

...

For Emile Durkheim, founder of modern sociology as an academic discipline, the principal cause of the progress of the division of labor is what he coined "organic solidarity"—as opposed to primitive societies which are characterized by a "mechanical solidarity" that is based on resemblance.

"Each organ, in effect, has its special physiognomy, its autonomy. And, moreover, the unity of the organism is as great as the individuation of the parts is more marked."

Durkheim rejects the utilitarian explanation of division of labor by gains in efficiency. Instead he introduces the idea of a "moral density" between previously unrelated social units and the emergence of a new "conscience collective".

Besides the highly problematic analogy of society as a biological organism Durkheims theory of the division of labors draws from two sources that seem constitutive for the emergence of modern humanities:
- the binary opposition of primitive versus civilized society which is inseparably linked with 19th century colonialism
- the direct transposition of Darwins "struggle for survival" to the idea of economic competition as the mediating mechanism between a growing social volume and advances in the division of labor.

...

The separation between manual and intellectual labor is constitutive for industrial capitalism: The separation of those who work "with their hands" and those who work with their "brain" is the fundamental proposition of the class society.

Alfred Sohn Rethel sees the division of manual and intellectual labor in close correspondance with the real abstraction of the commodity form and the epistemological implications of a philosophical tradition that understands thinking as a product of thinking and ultimately seperates between theory and practice and opens up the gap between conception and execution.

The exchange commodities goes along with an abstraction from the specific goods. Only the value of these goods is important. This abstraction is called 'real abstraction' because it takes place without a conscious effort, whether anybody is aware of it or not is of no importance. "People do not know it but they do it" (Marx). Sohn-Rethel argues that the real abstraction of the commodity form to be the real basis of formal and abstract thinking. All of Kant's categories such as space, time, quality, substance, accident, movement and so forth are implicit in the act of exchange.

Sohn-Rethel sees the transcendental unity of self-consciousness as an intellectual reflection of 'the form of exchangeability of commodities underlying the unity of money and the social synthesis'.

...

Adolf Eichmann, the manager of the logistics of the masstransports of European Jews to the extermination camps during World War 2 has been considered as the personification of the specialisation of labor in industrial capitalism and the inherent collapse of morality.

Rony Brauman and Eyal Sivan have edited the archive footage of the trial as their award winning docuemntary "The Specialist—portrait of a modern criminal". When Eichmann was brought to court in Israel in 1961 his line of defense was built on denying any legal responsibility for the deportations to the death-camps although Eichmann is referring to his reputation as a "specialist" in his field of all the logistics regarding expatriation, expropriation, and deportation of Jewish people.

In her report from the trial for the magazine "New Yorker" Hannah Arendt coined the expression of the "banality of evil". In Eichmann she did not discover a lack of empathy, as many other observers, she detected no stupidity, rather thoughtlessness.

It seems that the specification of knowledge and its celebration in managerialism coincides with a collapse of thinking since the fragmented action evacuates itself of any responsibility or even meaning.

Besides the massive proliferation of all sorts types of subjectivity related to the specialist (like the TV-expert, the nerd, the indian IT expert, just to name a very few) within culture industry we can encounter the opposite in the realm of production: A re-injection of individual creativity, overall responsability, forced collective liability, group or peer-pressure in ever smaller, isolated units of production under the banner of teamwork and co-operation.

...

Facing its increasing political irrelevance the official marxist debate in the course of the

20th century has more or less systematically shifted the focus from a materialist analysis of the division of labor towards phenomena of the superstructure: the culture industry, consumer society, society of spectacle etc.

What we experience today as "creative industries" is the reintegration of all sorts of practices that have not been considered productive under the reign of a new social division of labor. Political theory and organizing practices, have to re-address the issues of political economy in an significantly extended version.

How would it look like if instead of reasoning about the essence of immaterial production or the very character of creative industries one would investigate contemporary forms of the division of labor in postindustrial production processes?

1 At the first sight an increased level of control seems to be the ultimate purpose of a technical division of labor today.
2 While the segmentation of the work process in industrial production lead to an evacuation of meaning, in so-called immaterial production it is the other way around: meaning needs to be resampled through the re-collection of isolated practices under capitalist command or in more friendly words: co-operation. It is the proprietary code itself which does not only regulate access to the means of production and the repoduction of the productive forces, but establishes itself as a goal on its own.

The decomposition of the factory and the break-up of its theatrical unity of location, time, and story line have produced a new social division of labor that reflects that decomposition. The technical division of labor is sourced out to individual mini-entrepreneurial units with various split occupations across time and space.

The molar segmentations of the traditional division of labor that was based on reducing complexity, decreasing the knowledge that is needed for the steps of production is replaced by a rather molecular segmentation. The linear dramaturgy of the assembly line has turned into a transversal organization of work without an end or any limit.

This should lead us to research other divisions of labor beyond the technical and social division of labor. For example, the intensified fordist production in free trade zones expresses a global division of labor that runs parallel to colonial exploitation in the 19th century by providing ressources like cheap labor force on which the boom of the creative industries relies; gender-specific divisions of labor that have overhauled the fordist model of the small family, and hence demand new, migrant domestic labor.

...

If "division of labor is limited by the extent of the market" (Adam Smith) and the number and relative density of the population is a necessary condition for the division of labor

(Karl Marx) it is as urgent as obvious that an analysis of the social division of labor today neesd to open up a new perspective on the effects of both, migration movements, as well as new information and communication technologies that have emerged in the end of the 20th century.

The ongoing lament about the precarization of labor provides if any, then only very superficial insight on the results of a massive reconfiguration of the work process. A radical political theory and praxis need at least attempt to get to the root of the problem and investigate a new division of labor that occurs as a response to the change in the mode of production.

At the same time, the booming praise and worship of the common appears as unadulterated kitsch. Instead of indulging in utopianism, rather than proclaiming an alleged commonality, that would exist a-priori to the hostile conditions of the postmodern workplace, a political project has to reflect how exactly one mode of production is superseded by another, the division of labor is altered, and the understanding of what constitutes fulfilling self-activity is redefined.

In the same way as the concept of proletarian solidarity was raising against the fragmentation and segmentation of workers subjectivity at the assembly line, an upgraded version is to be developed that would be capable of resisting the new social division of labor in postindustrial production or even propagating a new workerism of the creative industries. A concept of collaboration, as a refusal of co-operation, based on the experience that the only thing we have in common might be the fact that we have nothing in common.

The concept of "imaginary property" is situated at the crossing of two axes: Images and an image production that become increasingly a matter of proprietarization, since the expansion of the capitalist accumulation towards image production is no longer limited to the frontiers of certain media or technologies (like movie industry) but sets out to colonize the entire realm of imagination. This axis intersects with a process of accelleration in which the very notion of property itself becomes more and more a matter of imagination (as we experience it today in the crisis of education).

In terms of division of labor that means that the real appropriation, the relation of the laborer to the means of production by which the transformation of nature is undertaken, needs to be understood as a over-appropriation of the real (the production of images), while the relations of production, the exercise of economic ownership, the control of the access to the means of production becomes more and more imaginary or in other words: indiscernible in terms of what is real and what is not real.

In the field of design we encounter the chance to virtually undo the separation between intellectual and manual labor. It is not only because design may be situated in a grey zone between theory and practice. It is rather because of the double role, that characterizes design in its intrinsic relation to both the technical and social division of labor which is both subject to processes of design as well as shaping the very work of the designer. And this is by no means about an omnipresence and omnipotence of design, on the contrary:

PROPOSAL

The concrete proposal at the end of this very preliminary collection of material and associated thoughts is the following:

The question of a new division of labor needs to be addressed simultaneously radically practically as well as radically theorretically. A framework needs to be invented that can facilitate a wide range of experiments from research to campaigning. It could be exemplified by a "design-union" which is both: a think tank for the future of self-organization in the creative industries directly connected to an organizing campaign. It is about designing a union and at the same time a union for designers.

KOERT VAN MENSVOORT

RAZORIUS GILLETUS — CONFESSIONS OF A SUCKER FOR INNOVATION

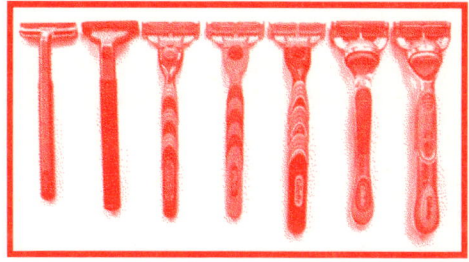

Razorius Gilletus (seven generations)

I got my first razor when I was fifteen. It consisted of two blades on a simple metal stick and I remember it gave me a really close and comfortable shave. In the twenty years that have passed since my first shave, I've used seven different models of razors. This morning I shaved myself with the <u>Gillette Fusion Power Phantom</u>, a rather heavy, yet ergonomically designed battery-powered razor that looks like a bit like vacuum cleaner and has five vibrating blades with an aloe strip for moisture. So what happened? A story about design, technology, market and evolution.

First, a personal disclaimer (in case you were wondering): Yes, I agree shaving technology was already sufficiently developed when I got my first razor twenty years ago. Already in 1975, shortly after the <u>Gillette Trac II</u> razor—the first two-bladed men's razor—was introduced, its excessive design was parodied on the US Television show Saturday Night Live. The creators of the satirical television program played on the notion of a two bladed razor as a sign of the emerging consumption culture and made a fake commercial parody for a fictitious razor with the ridiculous amount of three (!) blades, emphasizing the gullible consumer believing and buying everything shown on TV. Naturally, the comedians of Saturday Night Live could not fathom that three-bladed razors would become a reality on the consumer market in the late 1990s. Let alone that they could anticipate that I would shave myself with a five bladed razor this very morning. Welcome in the twenty-first century, folks: No we don't travel in spaceships... but we do have five bladed razors!

Fortunately, it is still possible to buy brand new blades for my very first razor model today. These older blades are not only cheaper—they are sold in a box of ten pieces for less money than a box of blades fitting the latest model, which contains only four cassettes. The older blades are also more durable. And yet, in the years that have past since my first shave, I bought over a dozen different razors—

I honestly have to confess I've bought some models of the competing brand as well. So, why did I buy this whole collection of razors over the years? Perhaps it is because I am the type of person who is keen on new things: I am a sucker for <u>innovation</u>.

COPY PASTE MIX BREED DELETE EVOLVE

Before we analyze my own behavior as a buyer, let's first study the razors themselves. If we look at the development of razor technology over time, we can discern quite some similarities with evolutionary development as we know it from the biological world:

1 Every new model builds upon the properties of the previous model.
2 Successful alterations are preserved in future generations, whereas unsuccessful alterations become obsolete.
3 The shift from functional technologies, like a pivoting head, to seemingly functionless aesthetics of the newer models, only changing in color and having no other purpose than to stand out amidst competing razor models, remind us of the exuberant tail of a male peacock.
4 The unique click-on systems for replacement blades on different models resemble biological immune systems withholding

intruders from entering and feeding on your environment.

5 There are even different survival strategies being tested, which over time may even result in separate species—think of the parallel branches in the more recent models that come <u>with</u> and <u>without</u> a battery. Apparently the marketers weren't sure whether the future will belong to electric or non-electrical shaving and decided to place their bets on both strategies—and yes, I confess: I bought both of them.

INTELLIGENT DESIGNER

Now it may seem quirky, corny even, to consider the development of razors from an evolutionary perspective. After all, these are industrial products assembled in factories. Yet I propose to look at them as the result of an evolutionary process. I can already hear your objections: "These razors didn't evolve, people designed them! How can that be an evolutionary process?" Well, allow me to elaborate—and this is where we learn something about our symbiotic relation with technology. Indeed it is true that all the individual razors were created by engineers and designers. However, if we look at the design of the whole series of razors as it developed throughout my shaving-career, it will be difficult to pinpoint one creator. Where is that one big mind, that 'intelligent designer' responsible for the transformation of the razor from a simple blade on a stick to a five bladed electric razor?

Obviously, many designers and engineers have been involved over the years in the creation of my razors. There can be no doubt that these are all descent and friendly people — with good incomes too — but what more are these creators of the individual models than little cogs in the eternal Gillette Corporation? Calling them engineers and designers is arguably too much credit for the work they do, as they merely draw up the sketches for the next razor model of which one can already predict the 'innovative' new properties: it will be a slight variation on the current model with some additional nanotech-sharpened blades, an extra moisterizing strip, an anti-slip grip or perhaps even a customizable color scheme. The razor designers don't seem to have a lot of space for truly creative design work. It's not like they are in a position tocontemplate the meaning and origins of shaving, in order to reinvent how this ancient ritual can be improved upon. Like bees in a beehive their work is determined by the logic of the larger corporate structure. The seat of that one great "intelligent designer" steering the entire development of shavers over time is empty. The larger design gesture emerges from the closely interrelated forces of the consumer market, technological affordances and of course the competition — think of the Wilkinson brand that first introduced a four bladed shaving system, thereby forcing Gillette to answer with a <u>five</u> bladed system. Considered together, these contextual influences constitute a sort of ecosystem, which (again) closely resembles the environmental forces known to play a part in the evolutionary development of biological species.

EVOLUTION, BUT NOT AS WE KNOW IT

Of course there are also arguments against this evolutionary view on the development of razor technology—so let's consider both sides of the coin. The most common objection is that "people play a role in the process, and therefore it cannot be evolution." This reasoning is tempting,but it also positions people outside of nature—as if we are somehow placed outside of the game of evolution and its rules would not apply to us. There is no reason to believe that this is the case: after all, people have evolved just like all other life forms. The fact that my razors are dependent on people to multiply is also not without precedent. The sameholds nowadays for many domesticated fruits like bananas, as well as a majority of the cattle on our planet. Moreover, we see similar symbiotic relationships in "old" nature: just think of the flowers that are dependent on bees to spread their pollen.

Another objection might be that my razors cannot be the result of an evolutionary development because they are made of metal and plastic and not a carbon-based biological species. This argument is supported by the assumption that evolution only takes place within a certain medium: carbon-based life forms. A variation of this argument states that evolution only takes place if there are genes involved—as is the case with humans, animals and plants. This way of thinking exemplifies a limited understanding of evolution, as it is a mistake to constrain it to a specific medium rather than to understand it as a general principle. In fact, the genetic system of DNA underlying our species is itself also a product of evolution—DNA evolved from the less complex RNA system as a successful medium of coding life. There is no reason why evolutionary processes could not transfer themselves to other media: Richard Dawkins already proposed "memes" as a building block of cultural evolution and Susan Blackmore suggested "temes" as building blocks for technological evolution.

In the end, the question we should ask ourselves is whether the environmental forces of economy and technology are at least equally or perhaps even more important for the evolution of razor technology than the design decisions made by the "inventors" of the individual models. I am rather sure this is the case and hence I propose to consider the development of razors as a truly evolutionary process—not metaphorically, but as reality. The species it brought into being we will call: <u>Razorius Gillettus</u>. It is just one of the numerous new species emerging within the techno-economical system—and it is evolving fast.

TECHNODIVERSITY IS INCREASING

Once we agree to perceive the development of razor technology as an evolutionary process, let's zoom in a bit on our own role in the evolutionary game. How would it be possible to imagine our relation with <u>Razoritus Gilletus</u> and its numerous fellow evolving technospecies? Are we like the bees—who feed themselves with nectar from flowers and in return spread their pollen, enabling the flowers to reproduce—heading towards a symbiotic relationship with the technosphere, which feeds upon our labor and creativity, and in return gives us <u>Razorius Gilletus</u>? Should we take pride in our role as catalysts of evolution, propagators of a technodiversity unlike the world has ever seen, being the one and only animal that transfers the game of evolution into another medium? We can. Yet, like in every symbiotic relationship, we should also inspect whether both parties are receiving an equal share of the deal. And although I did buy all these razors and they have been providing me with an ever-smoother-closer shave throughout my life, I am not entirely sure about that.

INNOVATION WITHOUT A CAUSE

To many of what we tend to call "innovations" are merely directed at increasing the growth and well-being of the technosphere—bigger economy, bigger corporations, more technological devices—rather than actually improving the lives of people. Indeed my latest shaver does shave just that tiny bit more smoothly than the previous model. Yet, if you would ask me if the device has "innovated" my life, I would have to answer no.

Let's face it: the new razors from Gillette are primarily created for the sake of the Gillette Corporation: higher turnover, more profit, more shareholder value. That's not a bad start, as good business provides people with good jobs and steady incomes, which allow them to live a happy live—and buy more razors. So far it's a win-win situation. Yet, the abundant production of all these devices also deploys an amazing amount of resources, putting quite some pressure on the biosphere—remember that good old nature that used to surround us before the emerging of the technosphere? We should not be naive about the fact that corporations—I know they'll tell you otherwise—do not intrinsically care all that much about the well-being of the biosphere. Being able to breathe clean air is simply not important for <u>Razorius Gillettus</u>, as it has a completely different digestive system. Clean air is only a requirement for carbon-based life forms like algae, plants, birds, polar bears, and of course people.

CATALYSTS OF EVOLUTION

So how to continue? I am the first to concur that there is a certain luster to the development of <u>Razorius Gillettus</u>. The notion that human activity is causing the rising of such a peculiar new species and that we are now co-evolving toward a shared future is intriguing to say the least. I wonder what Charles Darwin would have thought of this. Perhaps he would have pointed at the serious risks involved in this evolutionary leap. Certainly, our awareness of our own role as "catalysts of evolution" has yet to mature. It is a quite responsible job description we have got our hands on there. If we feel we are not fit for the job, we would do better to grow our beards and return to our caves. Which is a possibility, perhaps. At least some people have proposed we should do that. However, trying to turn back the clock of civilization would also be a denial of what it means to be human, or at least it exemplifies a cowardice toward the unknown. On the other hand, a purely techno-utopist attitude of 'letting grow' will expectedly also not be in the longtime benefit of humanity and our fellow biosphere-dependent species, as we run the risk of becoming obsolete altogether.

The mature thing to do in our position as catalysts of evolution is to develop a stewardship that focuses on maintaining a balance between both the declining biosphere and the emerging technosphere—between old nature and next nature. Toward an environment in which both can find a place and live in relative harmony. Now, I am not claiming that it will be easy. But if we would able to do that, we would have something to be truly proud of.

KOEN VERMEIR

THE MARKETS AND DESIGN

What are the effects of the economic crisis on the design industry? Are the excesses in the financial industry mirrored in some way by excesses in the creative industry? Do these excesses point at a fundamental flaw in capitalism and would there be a similar fundamental flaw in the technological deterministic prophecy of design enticed by the promise of progress? If we want to curb these excesses, how will life after the crisis look like? These are some of the questions I was asked to reflect on. In this text, I will try to shed some light on the curious relationship between capitalism and design and its consequences for the creative industry after the crisis.[1]

For a very long time already, technology and economy have stood in a close relationship with each other. The development of new

---
(1) Many of the thoughts in this paper were developed in discussions with Helga Aichmaier, and I would like to express my gratitude to her.

technologies has inspired new economic attitudes and structures at least since the middle ages. Trade secrecy, the creation of institutional structures such as guilds that served to protect technical knowledge, and the creation of legal structures such as patents and copyright to protect intellectual property are medieval developments, while more recently, innovation has become a crucial component of national economies. It is exactly in this respect that many thinkers have considered technology essentially as market friendly, in contrast to science, which is based on the values of openness and disinterestedness.

Andy Warhol as an icon of mass culture: his artwork at the same time criticizes and uses mass production, making him a millionaire in the process.

One of the striking effects of the rise of capitalism and industrialization has been the design and mass production of artifacts. It is well known today that objects produced <u>en masse</u> push down the costs of production, increasing the margins and profit of a company. On the other hand, low cost production has also led to affordable and good quality products and technologies, allowing even more people to increase their possession of desirable objects and to participate in consumer culture. In this way, the middle classes came into existence, and capitalism did not only generate the mass production of objects, but a veritable mass culture. One can lament these changes and dream of an artisanal pre-modern past, but it would be naive to think that we can go back to a pre-modern situation. Even the creation of artisanal objects or the production of unique objects by exclusive designers is no return to a pre-modern past but rather constitutes a distinct and decisively capitalist high-end economy of luxury.

Ron Arad's 'recycled' or 'ready-made' Rover chair from 1981, using a scrap yard seat from a Rover 200 car mounted on a frame of Kee-Klamp scaffolding originally designed in the 1930s, produced by One Off. Although a rather exclusive product, it was especially his later designs that employed labor intensive techniques, making them costly and exclusive. Arad consciously distanced himself from mass-produced designs.

Notwithstanding the inevitability with which current day capitalism clothes itself, especially after the deficit of competing ideologies, the financial and economic crisis of the last years has led people to put serious question marks behind capitalism. According to the current new consensus, uncontrolled capitalism is unstable. The last two economic crises have showed that capitalism needs regulation if the economy is not to degenerate in excessive behavior and if the markets are not to froth in irrational exuberance. Because the penetration of the economy into almost all spheres of modern life, these excesses of the financial industry have generated equivalent excesses in other practices. In this essay, I will look at the correspondence between excesses in the financial industry and in the design or creative industry.

The excesses of the financial crisis that led to the current recession (2008–?) can be characterized by a drive for profit for the sake of profit. This drive for profit led financial companies to take excessive leverage. They borrowed enormous amounts of money to invest in strongly growing but risky investments.[2] This meant that there were no hard assets, no substance but only debt standing behind these investments, so these companies would not be able to repay their loans if their investments went sour and decreased in value. In fact, it turns out that the financial industry was gambling with someone else's money. They were using the same money repeatedly to make more investments, turning $1 into $2, $3, even $10 of investments, by increasing the leverage. The real ingenuity of Wall Street was to repackage and sell these investments to other parties in order to distribute the risks. The idea was that they would be able to keep most of the profits, but that the risks were taken over by others (for a much too low risk/reward ratio, it now turns out). These structured products were so complicated that no one could really understand what they contained. They were constructed to generate trust, looking as if almost no risk but still a decent return were involved. In the end, these financial products were nothing but a façade, constructed to sell easily on the unsuspecting financial markets.[3]

In the design and creative industry we can find similar structures of excess. Instead of profit for the sake of profit, excess in the design industry is characterized by the idea of innovation for the sake of innovation—newness for the sake of newness. Often, as in the case of leveraged profit, there is nothing substantial behind a new product. The product is not new but only put into a new set of clothes. Instead of the reuse of the same dollar, multiplying itself virtually, in the design industry it is <u>design ideas</u> that are used over and over again; designs are repackaged multiple times and sold as innovations. Also in the design industry, risks are distributed to other parties, such as investors, producers, users and consumers. There is always a risk of failure inherent in the innovative process, such as a market failure or a technological failure, due to a wrong assessment of consumer groups or

---

(2) Leverage means that for every $10 a financial company has in assets, for instance, they would borrow an extra $90 to invest. If the investment would yield 20%, they would book a profit of $20 on the total investment. On the original amount of $10, this corresponds to a profit of 200%. The problem, of course, is if the investment decreases with 20% in value, there would only be $80 left, and they still would have to repay the borrowed $90 (with interest). This means that they would loose all their assets and would still be in debt for more than 100% of their original assets.

(3) Interestingly, design can be used to generate this trust. See e.g. Irini Athanassakis (2008) <u>Die Aktie als Bild: Zur Kulturgeschichte von Wertpapieren</u>. Berlin: Springer. In this book, it is shown how the visual design of stock certificates should convey a sense of security and trust.

due to the use of an inferior material. Finally, pretense and façade have become increasingly rampant in the creative industry. In order to win a competition for a major project, appearance is often more important than substance. Designers render beautiful images to entice the jury, but these are just simulacra. The images are useless in the real design practice and there is little substance behind them. By now, companies have emerged that specialize in create these façades, behind which there is only an empty box instead of a brilliant new design. This is maybe most clear in architecture design, but with the rise of virtual reality, this becomes a dominant practice in other domains of design.

Computer rendered image of a museum building in the Bristol harbor, redesigned to contain high end lofts, from the art project The Good Life (see below). This virtual image, and the accompanying marketing film, are meant to help imagining 'the ultimate in urban living' and wet the appetite of investors and clients.

The delusion that guides the ideology of capitalism is the idea of economic growth that can continue infinitely. A similar delusion, the idea of progress that can continue infinitely, determines the ideology of design and technological development. (These delusions are "modern" in a paradigmatic sense, because they presuppose a linear time that stretches into infinity, instead of the circular or limited time imagined in pre-modern societies.) Normally, profit and innovation go together with growth and progress respectively. They have come to be seen as the indicators of growth and progress and they signify success. If growth and progress can continue into infinity, the same should be expected from profit and innovation. Should we then be surprised that these ideologies lead to the excessive but unstable behavior that aims at generating profits, even if there is no growth, and that aims at generating innovations, even if there is no progress? The idea of an infinite progress generates a desire for continuous innovation. It generates a dynamic that, as soon as real progress halts, innovation for the sake of innovation continues as a sort of simulacrum. In the face of an unreasonable demand of ever increasing growth and progress, profit and innovation, which were originally only indicators, have separated themselves from their source. Profit and innovation have become independent ideals, and here success can still be achieved by smart financial/designing constructions and marketing strategies, even if growth and progress is lacking. These increasing profits and innovations have even generated a false sense, an illusion of growth and progress. The decoupling of profit and innovation from growth and progress is unstable and is responsible for the excesses that led to the current economic crisis.

Despite the close connection between capitalism and design and the similarity between their excesses, the economy, and especially neo-liberal capitalism, is not intrinsic to design. Other worlds, in which design has nothing to do with capitalism or even the economy, are possible. History shows that inventors from the classical era, such as Archimedes, were not guided by economic incentives. Furthermore, design does not have to be guided by ideals of progress and invention. In certain periods during the middle ages, novelty and innovation were often considered as bad, depending on the circumstances. Especially novelty for the sake of novelty was condemned as a vice. Instead, people valued tradition and skill as important virtues. Nevertheless, important technical breakthroughs were achieved in these periods. This indicates that design has its own internal norms that are separate from issues related to the markets and capitalism. Maybe technology has even its own, autonomous development as some philosophers have maintained. Instead of the innovation for the innovation, enforced on designers by market forces, design might have its own internally governed dynamics of innovation that had been lost during its enslavement to capitalism.

The recent economic crisis has brought to the fore the role of the markets in different areas of our life. It has made clear the instability of the neo-liberal ideology of infinite growth as well as the excesses of techniques that generate profit for the sake of profit, into infinity. This situation has made us critical and skeptical of market influences, and makes us imagine other worlds. It also makes us imagine the market as an external force that is able to corrupt the world of design, innovation and technological development.

I can see two plausible reactions to the economic crisis in the world of design. One reaction is pragmatic. The availability of fewer investor funds as well as the reduced financial means of the consumer will generate a fight for capital and increased competition among designers and producers. The urge may be to reduce cost (by searching creative solutions or by employing inferior materials for instance) or to refine marketing strategies to win out from competitors. Another approach would be to develop strategies to find the new interesting niches for designers in a post-crisis world. Many consumers will have to scale down on cost but do not want to give up quality. Therefore, products fitting into this category might find their market share increasing (exclusive and unique luxury design might lose out from the high-end quality mass produced objects, for instance). Designers and developers go into survival mode and try to exploit the new, more difficult conditions of a post-crisis economy.

A second reaction is idealist. The designer could reject the dominance of market forces and focus on the internal dynamics of innovation. This possibility is expressed for instance by Anthony Dunne and Fiona Raby: "Design today is concerned primarily with commercial and marketing activities but it could operate on a more intellectual level. It could place new technological developments within imaginary but believable everyday situations that would allow us to debate the implications of different technological futures before they happen."[4] This position emphasizes the cathartic effect of the crisis. Corruptive forces are rejected in favor for a renewed focus on the basic norms of the design process. The basic motivation for many designers was not financial or economic but was grounded in the desire to create new meaningful, aesthetic and useful objects. Many design teachers advise students to follow the internal dynamics of their thought in developing new objects or buildings, reinvigorating their desire to be inventors or artists. The current crisis could lead some to return to what they see as the purer roots of their profession, which are considered to be far from the corruptive influences of financial interests.

Many designers see design as the practice of problem solving. Someone comes with a problem and the designer solves it. This is a purely internalist view. It represents the view of the innovator, focusing on the creation of the artifact. Technical problems and solutions display their own kind of logic and dynamics. Such a view can easily lead to an idea of technological determinism.[5] (These ideas are explored in more depth in the text <u>Design and Technological Determinism.</u>) A more complex view of the design process, which also assists in eluding the trap of technological determinism, includes the user's perspective on technical artifacts as well as social factors. First, the meaning of an artifact is not determined by the intentions of the designer, but is constituted in its use. Meaning is use, as Wittgenstein had it. Second, the development, as well as the various uses of artifacts, are to a large extent influenced by social factors. Social contexts are therefore crucial for understanding technologies. This of course includes economic concerns and market forces.

As a reaction to the economic crisis, it would be tempting to reject the role of economic interests in the development of technologies. It is indeed important that design does not become the slave of financial interests and the gambles of venture capitalists. On the other hand, the creative industry needs the financial markets. Many designs could never be realized without funding for its development and without a considerable investment for production. But if the very meaning of an artifact is

---

(4) Design for Debate, www.dunneandraby.co.uk/content/bydandr/36/0 [accessed on 13.10.2009].

(5) One good example is the course handbook <u>Engineering: The Nature of Problems</u> at the Open University (openlearn.open.ac.uk/course/view.php?id=3071)

constituted by its use—and in capitalist mass culture this means by its consumption—the markets have an even more fundamental role. What would an artifact without users be? And today, the inevitable link between the designer and the user in a globalized economy is the market.

In modern societies, direct contact between the designer and the actual user is very rare or only takes place on a personal and incidental level.[6] The design markets look for an outlet for newly developed technologies, they sound user groups for their needs, they even create desires and needs in the consumers, and they take care of the actual distribution of goods. (The markets are not necessary in every form of design. An artist might make a dysfunctional object that would not sell by a normal design market, maybe he or she meant it as a critique of market forces, but then again, there is also an art market for such artifacts.) Of course, the connection between markets and designers and users is not direct and unproblematic. Marketeers may imagine impossible technologies and they might see imaginary desires and needs in society, but they nevertheless play an indispensable mediating role. This model, which we can call the "design system," is of course still much too simplified. There are many more roles involved (design strategy, planning, engineering, fabrication, marketing, brand strategy, public relations, packaging, advertising, trend gauging, trend creation and an infinity of different users) and it is important to see that all these roles co-constitute technologies, and negotiation takes place at each link of this chain. Simplified, however, its dynamics can be usefully characterized by the three general elements, design process, use and the market, which together constitute the "design system".

Panamarenko's designs of flying machines that cannot fly: a dysfunctional artifact as a fashionable object on the art market.

The point that I want to make in this essay is that each of these elements, design, use and the market has its own internal logic, norms and goals. Of course, there are many goals that can be taken into account, depending also on contextual factors, but there are only a few central goals that come close to defining a practice. The central goals of design, use and the market can be summarized as <u>innovation</u>, <u>functional and aesthetic use</u> and <u>profit</u> respectively. In the ideal situation, all these goals are aligned. Indeed, a novel functional and aesthetic product will be a pleasure to use and

---

(6) Prototype testing is of course taken very serious by industrial designers, but they can only work with test persons who are ideal type users, and only special target groups are taken into account. Real uses are infinitely richer than the intended uses tested by the test persons.

see, and it will sell well. But, of course, these goals cannot always be fulfilled simultaneously. If these goals are not in alignment, they have to be negotiated and a balance has to be found. One of the excesses that can occur is if the market component would win out exclusively. The markets and their financial clout can put a lot of pressure on other domains such as design, which might yield and give up their own internal logic, norms and goals in favor of economic factors and market interests.

But is should be noted that financial interests do not corrupt in a privileged way. I have already argued that innovation for the sake of innovation is also an excess that destabilizes design from the inside, so to speak. It is also possible that the exclusive preference for aesthetic goals results in excesses that make artifacts attractive but dysfunctional, which causes again imbalances between design, functional and aesthetic uses and the design markets. In order for the normal design system to function well, all the norms and goals of the different components should be negotiated and balanced.

As soon as we recognize this, it becomes clear that even the most reviled spearheads of capitalism can be a positive factor. Venture capitalism, for instance, is not necessarily bad. To the contrary, it makes many new developments possible that without its support would never come into existence. Venture capitalists make new green technologies or new medical treatments possible by funding the risky initial stages of development, but of course they also invest in new nuclear energy or pesticide development. In this way, they help changing the world in a good or a bad way. As Steven Shapin has recently shown, venture capitalists only get involved after careful calibration and negotiation of the goals and norms of everyone concerned.[7] Venture capitalists are interested in designers who are passionately involved with their innovations and who follow the internal logic of their work to find the most efficient and aesthetic designs. On the other hand, they also take care that the designer is able to let go his or her cherished brainchild when market rationality becomes important in producing and selling the product. They make sure that the designer's internal goal of inventing the perfect and ideal design will not come to dominate other goals, such as user's ease or the market goal of profit. In a way, they are striving towards the ideal alignment of norms as described above. Of course, excesses are always possible in which market goals come to prevail over all other goals, but in principle, venture capitalism involves an interesting process of negotiation between the relevant goals and norms of designers, users and markets.

---

[7] Steven Shapin (2008) The Scientific Life: <u>A Moral History of a Late Modern Vocation</u>. Chicago: Chicago University Press. See also Koen Vermeir, 'We zijn uit het oog verloren wat ons drijft om aan wetenschap te doen: interview met Steven Shapin' <u>Campuskrant</u> (KULeuven) 27/05/2009, p.9

Of course, only if people are aware of these conflicting norms and goals are they able to negotiate between them. It is therefore crucial to show the hidden forces that are often in play, and to raise awareness, for instance by education, art and criticism. <u>The Good Life</u>, for instance, an art project by Ronny Heiremans and Katleen Vermeir, questions in a subtle and ironic way the monetary interests involved in the development of the creative industry.[8] This includes, for instance, the role of artists, designers and cultural agencies in the gentrification of neighborhoods, with all its economic implications, such as the rising value of real estate and the resulting forced migrations of social classes to less regenerated areas. By making visible and subtly magnifying real life possibilities, they make spectators aware of the hidden mechanisms that drive much of our current society in general and the fashions of the creative industry in particular. <u>The Good Life</u> projects a marketing vision of an ideal life that is defined by consumption. The "promotional video" goes just over the edge of real marketing practices, showing the uncanny effects when marketing and financial interests start to dominate the most personal aspects of our lifestyle and life-world. Laying bare that our whole lifestyle and many of our desires might be generated by marketing strategies makes us question their authenticity and reflect about the excessive penetration of market forces in current culture.

An <u>awareness</u> of the often invisible processes behind design and technological development helps to make possible what I think is the most striking feature of the design process: the briefing, rebriefing and debriefing, or the negotiations between the different parties. This negotiation should not be confined to a to-and-fro between the desires of the client and the ideas of the designer, however. Given a more complicated picture with a complex dynamic between the various kinds of designers, users and market elements involved, this negotiation should involve all parties with their different goals, norms and strategies. An awareness of these often invisible processes makes it possible to include them in the negotiation process.

To conclude, I would like to point out that one of the new positive effects of the crisis might also have positive repercussions on the design process. There is a newly emerging sensibility and awareness for what are called externalities, and this could amount to a complete overhaul of capitalism itself. An externality is produced by a design system, but its effects are external to it. One example is a manufacturer of a new technological innovation which pollutes the environment by emitting toxic gasses and against which no sanctions are taken. By shifting away the negative effects of the production process to

---

(8) See www.thegoodlife-collection.com; see also www.in-residence.be.

the surrounding villages, the manufacturer is able to keep its costs low (and increase profit for the stockholder) and keep the products cheap (which is good for consumers). The real costs, such as the pollution and resulting health problems, are carried by actors outside the design system.[9] Financial analyst Jim Jubak explains that current capitalism is constantly at work rewarding producers and consumers who make as many of their costs into externalities as possible: "In effect, the market encourages producers and consumers to push costs from the private realm—where they have to come out of private pockets—to the public purse where everybody [including people who were external to the transaction] has to pick up the cost."[10] Regulators can make these externalities internal by forcing the manufacturer to install filters or to clean up the pollution, for instance. These regulative processes come increasingly to the fore, but with tackling problems like global warming, the world is for the first time taking up the problem of externalities on a global scale. Let us hope this effort succeeds and sets a precedent.

The design process involves hidden internalities as well as externalities. The designer, user and the narrow market of production and sales are not isolated from the broader world. The goals of <u>innovation</u>, <u>user's ease or pleasure</u> and <u>profit</u> that determined the design process should be amended with even more general values that involve moral, ecological and other concerns. I have argued that venture capitalists help changing the world, but they can do it for better or for worse, and this is of course not a trivial issue. Everyone in the design process should take their responsibilities in showing the externalities that are created and to include them in the negotiations of the design process itself.[11]

Also hidden internalities are important. The market goal behind a new publicly funded building or artwork might have been to increase the real estate value of the neighborhood and generate a profit for stakeholders. What seemed to be external to the design and development process was in fact internal but hidden and calculated by the market factors involved. These hidden internalities and externalities should be made visible and explicit, so that a variety of responsibilities become clear. Awareness of these processes makes it possible to include them in the negotiations, briefings and debriefings that are at the core of the design process. This might be the most important contribution of the economic crisis in creating a new kind of capitalism and a new design process that takes the dialectic of briefing and debriefing to a new level.

---

(9) See Gordon Tullock (2005) Public Goods, Redistribution and Rent Seeking, Edward Elgar Publishers. See also www.environmentbusiness.com.au/policy/0405-externalities.pdf for a call to undertake an in-depth analysis of the economic impacts of negative externalities and the role of technology.

(10) Jim Jubak, 'Time for capitalism to pay its way' October 6, 2009, money.ca.msn.com/investing/jim-jubak/article.aspx?cp-documentid=22101557

(11) For an example, see e.g. the cradle-to-cradle method of durable design propounded in William McDonough & Michael Braungart (2002) Cradle to Cradle – Remaking the Way We Make Things, North Point Press.

Velocipede, about 1868

Unzicker tricycle model, 1878

Standard Columbia Bicycle, 1881

Columbia Light Roadster Ordinary, 1888

St. George's New Rapid bicycle, 1889

Cleveland safety bicycle, 1899

NOTES ON DESIGN AND TECHNOLOGICAL DETERMINISM

Many designers see design as the practice of problem solving. Someone comes with a problem and the designer solves it. This is a purely internalist view. It represents the view of the innovator, focusing on the creation of the artifact. Technical problems and solutions display their own kind of logic and dynamics. Especially with hindsight, if we look at how the modern car, bike or airplane developed from their still unsophisticated predecessors, technical innovations often seem logical and almost inevitable (e.g., see the appended image of a genealogy of bicycles). We usually do not get to see the failed designs, or many of those that have fallen in disuse. Like in biology, there is a pervasive sense of teleology, even if this is not borne out by the facts. This internalist perspective has led to the view of technological determinism. Technological determinism involves two distinct ideas:

1. that technological development follows its own inner logic and
2. that technology determines how it is used, and therefore, that it has specific inherent effects on society. 'Die Sache hat uns in der Hand', as Musil puts it.[1]

The idea of technological determinism might appear alien to some designers, because it abstracts from the creative process of design with which they are occupied. We do not see the failed inventions and the paths of thought abandoned in the creative struggles of the designers.[fig.1] Nevertheless, only few designers reflect on the messiness and the opaque character of the creative process.[2] Contrarily, handbooks for design students often express a view that amounts to technological determinism. One good example is the course handbook <u>Engineering: The Nature of Problems</u> at the Open University, (http://openlearn.open.ac.uk/course/view.php?id=3071) and it is worthwhile to quote extensively from section 5.1.

The first sentence of this section reads: "Section 4 has looked at how we can follow a logical route or map, from the expression of a need, to arrive at possible solutions to a problem", expressing the idea of a logical route between problem and solution, from innovation to innovation, that is essential to the concept of technological determinism. In section 5 itself, the history of the development of the bicycle is studied as an example. The author starts, surprisingly, not with the design of Bicycles, but with their economic relevance:

> The modern bicycle frame is central to a huge international business, dominated by American and Chinese markets. In the USA, current estimates put the market at about 15 million bicycles per annum and, in an increasingly environmentally conscious society, the future looks pretty much guaranteed. In this context, the bike is a mature product in an established market, but at some point in history there were no bicycles and the first design must have been produced in order to meet a need.

This straightforward association with economic considerations shows nicely how much capitalism has become ingrained in design (see my accompanying text <u>Market and design</u>).

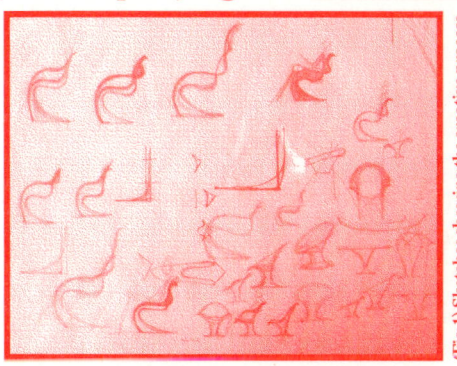

(Fig.1) Sketches showing the creative process of developing the "ideal chair", the Panton Chair by Danish designer Verner Panton, produced in collaboration with Vitra.

Next, the teacher leads us back to the eighteenth century in order to lay out for us the first

---

(1) Robert Musil (2009 ed.) <u>Der Man ohne Eigenschaften</u>. Rowohlt, p.32
(2) For a study of the creative process of design itself, see projects by Eikones and the Hochschule fur Gestaltung und Kunst (Basel) and the work of Helga Aichmaier.

logical steps in the development of the bicycle:
In fact, the first vehicle that worked with two wheels in a line (the very basic characteristic that came to define a bicycle) was introduced in France in 1791 with a non-steering front wheel, no pedals and a wooden horse's head! For its time, this 'bicycle' was an innovation, and unbelievably it didn't change much for the next twenty years or so. In 1817 a steerable front wheel was introduced (in Germany) and pedals made their first appearance in 1839 (in Scotland). The chain, the sprocket-driven rear wheel and equal-sized front and back wheels were added in England in the early 1880s and were followed by pneumatic tires, two- and three-speed hub gears and then derailleur gears before the turn of the century.

Each of these major changes came about through engineers finding solutions through innovation by context, but along the way there were literally hundreds of small innovations by development and numerous routine design improvements. For example, in 1879 Charles E. Pratt wrote in his handbook <u>The American Bicycler</u>:

"From 1868 until the present time the patented improvements have been numerous, and the mechanical details of construction have been thoroughly worked out, until the machine has become a marvel of ingenuity and of workmanship; and the modern bicycle has been developed to its present state of perfection in strength, lightness, ease of propulsion, certainty of control, and gracefulness of design and operation."

This is an accolade that would swell any engineer's head, but it implies that any advances since 1879 have been extraneous! A 1879 position reflecting technological determinism and an ideology of progress, where the current situation is seen as the culmination point and 'a state of perfection', is reinforced in a course by a design professor of the 21st century. Both authors give a striking expression of the evident logic, driven by an internal necessity, displayed in the historical development of the bicycle: first two wheels in a line, then a steer is added, later pedals are added, and finally equal-sized wheels, the chain, tires and gears are added, as if everything was lying ready in a toolbox. Interestingly, the professor also addresses the second aspect of technological determinism: its inherent effects on society:

An interesting aside to the technological advancement of the bike is in respect of the effect that engineering has on society. The bicycle is generally attributed as being pivotal in the liberation of women in the USA and Europe. Women in England were able to travel independently and in relative safety for the first time, particularly after Queen Victoria made it a socially acceptable practice by riding her tricycle alone in public. A postmistress in the USA, Amelia

Bloomer, designed the first trousers for women—bloomers—specifically for riding bikes. The same Amelia Bloomer went on to spearhead the Suffragette fight for women's right to vote in the USA.

The idea of technological determinism expresses the feeling that technological development follows an inevitable, almost autonomic track, which is often identified with "progress", but which is also sometimes seen as dangerous. Another element that invigorated the idea of technological determinism is the myth of the designer, that in getting the idea of an invention, a solution suggests "itself". It is a classical expression of the idea of genius: the solution to a problem is perceived as coming from the outside, it is a given. This also suggests that there is a solution out there, like a Platonic idea, waiting to be discovered or to be whispered by a muse. Lastly, the development of technology is now pursued on a world scale. Even if particular technological innovations are developed by particular individuals, there is a feeling that technology has detached itself from the individual and follows its own course. Technical possibilities will be explored, if not in the USA, then in China. Someone will try it out and develop it, fulfilling technology's internal logic. The atom bomb was in the cards, and from there, the H-bomb was inevitable. Even if we prohibit practices like human cloning, there is a widespread fear that someone will nevertheless try it out, maybe in a criminal organization or a rogue state. Technology is independent of its inventors, it seems, and the technical possibilities opened up by a new development will be explored and realized, wether we want it or not. Furthermore, the idea that technology is an autonomous force stems from the belief that somehow technology has gotten out of control and is following its own course, independent of human direction. This autonomy is not the strangeness of a different culture, but has the alienating character of an independent, inhuman agency.

This is a bizarre idea, given that technology is of our own making. I do not mean the notion that we have no control over what we have made, but rather the idea that we have no control over what we <u>will</u> make (i.e., what we will decide to make). Of course, what we create is dependent on human ingenuity, the state of current knowledge, and the available resources. But the idea is that technology exhibits its own dynamics as if it created itself (through us). This idea is an effect of a mix of other confused ideas, including the idea that the consequences of technology might be out of control, and the feeling of impotence vis à vis present-day institutions, which determine science and technology policy. Anonymous institutions, sometimes masking different pressure groups, decide on which research will get funding and which new technologies will be developed. Technological determinism is a view that results from a narrowed down perspective, focusing only on the creative process and the internal reasoning in design, and ignoring the users and the social role of technologies. Many of the negative effects of technology lamented by philosophers are, in fact, effects of the narrow and one-sided rationality of capitalism, utilitarianism, and globalization. Technology is not inhuman, unless our society and we ourselves have already become inhuman, and it is here that the humanists have their important task.[3]

The first idea of technological determinism can be countered by looking at the social and market forces that support and guide the developments of technologies. Even the creative process itself is inherently social, consisting of collaborations and borrowing elements from all sides of culture. The second idea of technological determinism is rebutted by taking a user's view on technical artifacts, and by recognizing that artifacts can be used in many ways, often unintended by the designers. Some uses are socially learned and sanctioned, while other uses come from hands-on experience with the object. These uses are not determined by a technology, but they are invited or suggested by it.

In a famous text, Pinch and Bijker elaborate the example of the "social construction" of the bicycle, in which different variants (such as the Facile, the Penny Farthing and the Xtraordinary) are discussed, together with the reasons why they received support and why they were suppressed in the end. In a related text, Kline and Pinch discussed the social construction of the automobile. In both cases, it becomes clear that there is a lot of interpretative flexibility on what should be characteristic of a good bicycle or a good car. Women argued that a good bicycle should be decent and safe, for instance, while men favored velocity, and the diversity of bicycles that were constructed in this early period reflected these predilections. These studies are particularly enlightening in showing that there were many different opinions possible in the development of technologies.[4]

I am not suggesting that technology is just a social construction, that it is inherently neutral and (when developed) that humankind fully determines its use and meaning. As Mazlish points out, many studies on technology end with the same sterile conclusion: technology can cause both good and evil; it is up to humankind to decide how and for which goals it will be employed.[5] Such a conclusion does not teach us anything, and will not help us to understand the power of technology. Tech-

---

(3) Bruno Latour is also proposing an alternative to technological determinism on the one side and social constructivism on the other side. In order to do this, however, he develops an ontology in which artifacts have real agency, intensions and goals. My account avoids such an exotic ontology.

(4) See Trevor Pinch and Wiebe Bijker, 'The Social Construction of Facts and Artifacts: Or How the Sociology of Science and the Sociology of Technology Might Benefit Each Other', in: <u>The social construction of technological systems: New directions in the sociology and history of technology</u>, ed. Wiebe Bijker, Thomas Hughes and Trevor Pinch (Cambridge, MA, 1987).

(5) Bruce Mazlish, <u>The Fourth Discontinuity. The Co-Evolution of Humans and Machines</u> (New Haven: Yale University Press, 1993), p.7

nology <u>does</u> have some kind of autonomy, and pragmatic theories fail to make this sufficiently clear. Artifacts are made for a certain purpose; they have a function and their design is styled according to that function. Pragmatists are correct in stating that nothing <u>compels</u> us to use an artifact according to its alleged function. We can use a brick as a hammer, or a hammer as a murder weapon. In this sense, an artifact (or any object) has no intrinsic meaning, and its meaning changes according to its use. However, the design of an artifact does limit its possible uses and often favors a specific use. We cannot use a hammer as a telephone to make appointments with others, nor can we use a chair as an oven to bake a cake.

Technology influences our lives in different ways, and we are not entirely free to determine its meanings by our use of it. <u>Technology is invitatory, co-directive and suggestive</u>; its different potentials can be actualized in different ways. It does not determine or compel us to a certain use, but it indicates and sometimes even "insists" on a way of use. These uses may go further than the "authorial intention," or the alleged function of an instrument, and in this way it can escape human control. Mobile phones and email are designed for users to be easily accessible and continuously in (potential) contact with the rest of the community. On the one hand, this has associations of "connectedness," "optimising" and "efficiency," supporting and enhancing business. On the other, always being "in touch" can have positive effects on sociability, but it has profound effects on our daily experience too. One often catches oneself checking emails or calling someone in almost every brief moment one is alone. These technologies seem to <u>lure</u> us into a certain pattern of use, and drastically alter our solitary experience or experience of waiting, for instance, which seems to be an intrinsic but unexpected part of their design; think also of computer game addicts or the phenomenon of the "child viewer" as unexpected "consequences" of computer and television. Possibly this aspect of technology also contributes to the idea that it acts as an "autonomous" force. This is already clear from the difficulty of using phrases like "technology lures" or "insists" without presupposing some kind of autonomy. Nevertheless, seeing this kind of autonomy as an inhuman power is wronheaded. It is true that technology disciplines us in many and sometimes unexpected ways, but this should rather be interpreted as potentialities, limitations and constraints in ways of use.

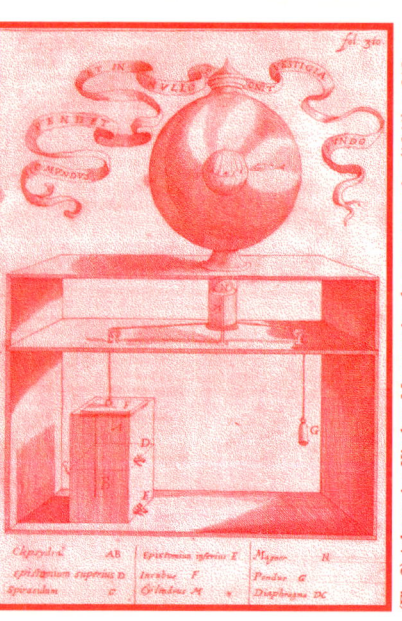

(Fig. 2) Athanasius Kircher, Magnes sive de arte magnetica (1641), p. 310

(Fig. 1) Athanasius Kircher, Magnes sive de arte magnetica (1641), p. 736

IMPOSSIBLE INSTRUMENTS AND TECHNOLOGICAL DETERMINISM

In this text, I will elaborate the example of a specific type of instruments, which might aptly be called "impossible instruments". These "impossible instruments" are border cases that question the concept of technological determinism and the idea of a teleology in design development. At the same time, they question the connection between design and the financial markets. Even if these artifacts seem incomprehensible and utopian today, they were meant as serious designs in earlier periods of history, and understanding them in their historical context poses a major challenge.

In 1641, a description and illustration of a curious instrument was published, as part of a huge scholarly tome on magnetism. It was a clock made from a sunflower plant which, put in a basin, would follow the movements of the sun.[fig.1] There were descriptions of other wondrous instruments in the book, but this one stood out in its singularity and evoked a controversy back in the seventeenth-century as well as in contemporary historical scholarship. The curious description of the construction of the clock can be paraphrased as follows.[1]

The sunflower is attached to a big cork (ABC), which serves as a big "vase" and holds the flower. The cork and sunflower are put in a large basin filled with water and are attached to a pivot in the middle. In this way, the sunflower can turn around its axis easily and without obstructions. Around the stem and root one can fasten woolen bandages, which, when let into the water, absorb it and feed the plant, so that the sun does not dry it up. By daybreak, the author explains, the sun will affect this machine, which is exposed to the open air. The sun attracts the heliotropic, or "sun-turning," flower because of the major efficacious virtues this plant possesses. The flower is not hampered by the earth anymore, and the face of the flower will turn itself swiftly to the face of the sun. In this way, the author claims, the flower circles the hours and a pointer (F) attached to the centre of the flower (T) will indicates the hour on the "clock dial" (DE) which is constructed around the flower.[2]

This concrete description of how to make a "botanical horoscope" and the corresponding detailed drawing come from Athanasius Kircher's <u>Magnes sive de arte magnetica opus tripartitum</u> (1641). In this book, the Jesuit philosopher, "linguist" and mathematician described the properties of magnetism, its various applications (in astronomy, natural magic, geography, navigation, etc.) and its hidden workings in the world. The botanical clock was part of this last section on the powers of magnetism which dealt with, for instance, the magnetism of the earth, the planets and the stars, but also with magnetic attraction in plants, medicine and music, and even with the magnetic nature of love and God.

Kircher argued that his newly invented clock indicated the time in an optimal way, because the pivot allowed the flower to turn unhampered towards the magnetic attraction of the sun. Heliotropism, Kircher thought, was a special instance of vegetal magnetism. This meant that the clock would even work at night (contrary to the common sundial), because the magnetic influence of the sun was not weakened by material barriers. On the other hand, Kircher admitted, there were also some disadvantages to the clock. A slight breeze would distort its movement, for instance. Furthermore, this vegetal clock would only last about a month before withering away. Therefore, Kircher proposed other clocks that worked by means of a similar "magnetic" principle.

---

(1) The example elaborated in this section is based on earlier research that was published as Koen Vermeir (2006) 'The Reality of Failure. On the interpretation of success and failure in (the history and philosophy of) science and technology' in S. Zielinski and D. Link (eds.) Variantology II. On Deep Time Relations of Arts, Sciences and Technologies. Cologne: Walter König. 335–360

(2) Athanasius Kircher, Magnes sive de arte magnetica (Rome, 1641), pp.736–737 (the image can be found between these two pages)

One clock worked by virtue of some kind of heliotropic material (purchased from a mysterious Arab in 1633) that Kircher propped upon a cork, similar to his "botanical horoscope". Accounts of Kircher's previous experiments and demonstrations as described in letters by contemporaries indicate that, from 1633 onwards, he had been experimenting with heliotropic roots and sunflower seeds, both of which supposedly turned towards the sun by means of a magnetic principle. These clocks were an improvement because they had a handy size and they could be protected by a glass case against the wind. On the other hand, the magnetic virtue inherent in the vegetable kernel of these clocks was often affected by the water in which it lay, and the clocks only lasted a few hours. Therefore, Kircher had devised a new kind of clock which was based on a magnet which, he suggested, turned with the sun by means of a similar heliotropic magnetic virtue. These imperishable clocks, he noted, were described in the section on magnetic natural magic in the same book.[3]

In this section, however, a hidden mechanism behind these magnetic clocks was exposed.[fig.2] It turns out that the clocks were in fact powered by a hidden system. Instead of a celestial magnetism, a water clock made a magnet revolve underneath the table, which made in its turn the magnet in the glass globe rotate. If his clocks made from sunflowers, sunflower seeds or other heliotropic roots were constructed by similar trickery, what are we to believe of Kircher's account of celestial and heliotropic magnetism? Should we believe Kircher's statement that he had constructed a clock out of a sunflower, much to the admiration and delight of the spectators? On the one hand, a clock constructed from a sunflower seems to make some sense, since the heliotropic movement of the sunflower has been noted by many. On the other hand, botanists and biologists today have pointed out that the sunflower only shows this motion as long as its flower does not bloom. From the moment the flower opens, the plant freezes, most often in an eastward direction, and this suggests that Kircher's instrument as depicted in his book would be of little use. On the other hand, there are indications that this happens because a part of the sunflower's stem stiffens and cannot turn anymore. In this case, Kircher's setup in which the sunflower is put in water might actually allow the sunflower to turn again!

Furthermore, we now believe that heliotropism is not a magnetic effect. It is an interaction between sunlight (esp. blue light) and certain parts of the plant. This means that the clock cannot work inside a house, when there are too many clouds or at night, just like a sundial.[4]

---

(3) A. Kircher, Magnes sive de arte magnetica (Rome, 1641), esp. pp.309–312 (section Horologiographia Magnetica) and 342–356 (section Magia Naturalis Magnetica). The picture can be found after p.310

(4) Maureen L. Stanton and Candace Galen, Blue light controls solar tracking by flowers of an Alpine plant. Plant, Cell and Environment 16 (1993): pp.983–989

So, even granted the fact that one might construct such a clock, of what use could it be? The case can even be made stronger for the clock made of a heliotropic root or seed. Can we, from a 21st century standpoint, believe in the possibility of a clock driven by the occult magnetic virtue of a sunflower seed? How should we assess the function and use of such "impossible" instruments that seventeenth century savants claimed to have constructed? Can we meaningfully refer to the success or failure of such instruments? Should historians describe Kircher as a fraud or a cheat? Or are there other ways to come to grips with this curious figure?

Kircher's oeuvre seems to resemble an illusionist theater in which nothing is what it seems, and his play with illusion and reality, with secrecy and openness, confuses the modern reader. One is tempted to laugh his inventions off as absurdities or monstrosities. Why would one want to make a clock out of a sunflower or a sunflower seed—especially if such an instrument could not possibly have worked? Looking back from the 21st century, we are tempted to side with Kircher's critics, such as René Descartes or Christiaan Huygens, but how did Kircher and his supporters look at the matter? Why would Kircher publicize and demonstrate his artifacts so widely, if he thought that they did not work and were worthless? Kircher's supporters clearly did not think that he or his clocks were failures, and they continued to edit and publicize his works.

In order to resolve some of these questions, it is helpful to look at the opinion of Kircher's contemporaries. By 1641, when his Magnes was published, Kircher had experimented with and demonstrated such clocks for a long time already. In 1633, Nicolas-Claude Fabri de Peiresc, a famous scholar and member of the republic of letters, had witnessed some of Kircher's demonstrations with vegetal and magnetic clocks in Avignon, and Father Linus, a fellow Jesuit, had constructed a similar magnetic clock in Belgium. At some moments in his examination of such clocks, Peiresc had suspected that there was trickery involved. One of Kircher's clock devices turned out to be nothing more than an ordinary compass, and to make it indicate the right time, one had to adjust it manually all the time. On the other hand, Peiresc was also fascinated by the theoretical implications of such an instrument and wanted to believe in its existence, or at least in its possibility. He thought that these clocks could be used in support of the heliocentric theory and he hoped to employ them in his attempts to get clemency for Galileo Galilei.

Peiresc set into motion his scholarly network and corresponded with Pierre Gassendi, Marin Mersenne, Peter Paul Rubens and others on this issue. Galileo himself was less taken in by this idea than Peiresc and politely indicated to him that in all probability the instrument functioned by means of a hidden mechanism. Descartes, informed by an enthusiastic Mersenne, reacted at first rather skeptical, although he did not judge the effect impossible. Years later, he would write to Huygens that clocks driven by sunflower seeds were merely tricks, as his own attempts at constructing one had been unsuccessful. In contrast, in Catholic countries, Kircher had a wide and enthusiastic readership with those who sided with the rhetoric of the Counter Reformation. It turns out that contemporary assessments of Kircher and his wondrous clocks were mixed. Kircher's message was only appreciated by some, while others rejected his work as charlatanry.

Despite misunderstandings about the aims and workings of instruments, the reactions of Peiresc and Mersenne illustrate that there was a multiplicity of views, apart from outright support or dismissal, and a close study of any controversy shows a historical density and richness that complicates any simple opposition between world views. I think that these strange artifacts as well as the differences in their reception by the historical actors make us question what 'working' means, as it seems that artifacts can "work" for different people in very different ways. Sociologists of technology are right in pointing out that the meaning attributed to an artifact is much more important for historical and sociological studies than what we might think of as the "actual working" or "functioning" of the artifact, which is in the end just <u>our</u> perspective on the artifact.

To think about "impossible artifacts" is productive for designers. It will help designers to step out of the dominant frameworks and ways of thought that govern our current society. Instead of being focused on current reality and the technologies that are present, impossible instruments help us to imagine different possibilities and different worlds. And this is what design is all about. While normal people live in reality, designers live in a world of possibilities. As the example of Kircher's clock suggests, a study of the history of technology, with its strange quirks, branched of developments and aborted innovations can be seen as a pool of possibilities, of thought experiments as well as real experiments, which make us aware that the world could have been different. We should be aware that contemporary reality is surrounded by possibilities, in the future as well as in the past. The idea that technologies could have been developed differently, contradicting the basic tenet of technological determinism, is liberating for the designer and helps him or her to imagine different possibilities.

TECHNOLOGICAL DETERMINISM 1

THE GAME
PLAYERS: 2+

GAME PREPARATION: PEN OR PENCIL AND PAPER.

THIS IS HOW THE GAME WORKS: MAKE ONE FORM IN ONE CONTINUOUS LINE WITHOUT BACKTRACKING. IF YOUR LINE MEETS AN ALREADY EXISTING LINE (YOUR OWN OR A LINE OF A PLAYER BEFORE YOU), YOUR TURN IS OVER. NOW THE NEXT PLAYER CONTINUOUS THE DRAWING.

AIM: TRY TO DESIGN AN ARTIFACT OR TECHNOLOGY. THE GAME ENDS WHEN YOU REACH AGREEMENT ON THE SUCCESS OF THE DESIGN.

ADVICE: DON'T LIMIT YOURSELF TO THE WORLD OF THE REAL BUT OPEN UP A WORLD OF POSSIBILITIES.

DIFFERENT VERSIONS:
1. PLAY THE GAME IN SILENCE
2. PLAY THE GAME WHILE DISCUSSING TECHNOLOGICAL POSSIBILITIES
3. INTERSECTING LINES ARE ALLOWED IF YOU WANT TO EXPRESS A 3D STRUCTURE

(USE DOTTED LINES FOR THE HIDDEN PART) E.G.:

TECHNOLOGICAL DETERMINISM 2

THE SEQUEL

PLAYERS: 2+

GAME PREPARATION: PEN OR PENCIL AND PAPER.

THIS IS HOW THE GAME WORKS: MAKE ONE FORM IN ONE CONTINUOUS LINE WITHOUT BACKTRACKING. IF YOUR LINE MEETS AN ALREADY EXISTING LINE (YOUR OWN OR A LINE OF A PLAYER BEFORE YOU), YOUR TURN IS OVER. NOW THE NEXT PLAYER CONTINUOUS THE DRAWING.

AIM: TRY TO DESIGN AN ARTIFACT OR TECHNOLOGY.

ADDITIONAL RULE: YOU HAVE TO BE ABLE TO MAKE SENSE OF THE DRAWING AND EXPLAIN THE ARTIFACT TO THE OTHER PLAYERS IF YOU ARE CHALLENGED TO DO SO.

HOW TO WIN: KEEP ADDING FORMS TO THE PICTURE, INCREASING THE COMPLEXITY OF THE ARTIFACT.

HOW TO LOSE: GIVE UP. IF YOU GIVE UP, YOU CAN CHALLENGE THE OTHER PLAYERS TO EXPLAIN THE ARTIFACT TO YOU, HOWEVER. (THEY SHOULD NOT HEAR EACH OTHER'S EXPLANATION, SO WHISPER OR USE PEN AND PAPER.) EVERY OTHER PLAYER THAT FAILS TO DO SO LOSES. IF THERE ARE NO OTHER PLAYERS LEFT IN THE GAME EXCEPT FOR YOURSELF, YOU WIN.

ADVICE: DON'T LIMIT YOURSELF TO THE WORLD OF THE REAL BUT OPEN UP A WORLD OF POSSIBILITIES.

TECHNOLOGICAL DETERMINISM 3

BICYCLES (ALSO AVAILABLE: CARS, AIRPLANES, …)
PLAYERS: 1 (OR MORE)

WHAT YOU NEED: THE ACCOMPANYING PICTURES OF BICYCLES.

AIM: TRY TO DISCOVER THE INTERNAL LOGIC OF THE DEVELOPMENT OF THE BICYCLE.

GOAL: ORDER THE ACCOMPANYING PICTURES OF HISTORICAL BICYCLES CHRONOLOGICALLY.

(YOU CAN CHECK HOW CLOSE YOU ARE ON:

WWW.AMERICANHISTORY.SI.EDU/ONTHEMOVE/THEMES/STORY_69_3.HTML)

Onomatopee 36
Research project
Design Mass

Managing & artistic director
Freek Lomme

Texts
Florian Schneider;
Koert van Mensvoort;
Koen Vermeir

Text editor
Vincent van Gerven Oei

Graphic design
Rob van den Nieuwenhuizen
& Jeremy Jansen

Exhibition design
Remco van Bladel

Printing
New Goff, Gent

Paper
Munken Print Cream;
Maco Satiné HV

Typeface
Larish Neue
(by Radim Peško);
Helwetica
(by Karl Nawrot)

Edition
550 copies

Supported by
Municipality of Eindhoven

We would like to thank Rob Ritzen, Bas van Loon, Hadas Zemer, Ron Eijkman

© 2010 Onomatopee and the authors

www.onomatopee.net
info@onomatopee.net

All rights reserved. No part of this publication may be reproduced, stored in a retrieval system, or transmitted in any form or by any means, electronic, mechanical, photocopying, recording or otherwise, without the prior written permission from the authors and the publisher.

ISBN 9-789078-454540

gemeente Eindhoven